Series Introduction

The Grattan Street Shorts series has been designed to showcase outstanding writing that does not fit neatly into conventional formats. It will include novellas, linked short stories, collected microfiction, long essays, fictocriticism and experimental memoir, and will feature the work of emerging writers particularly, but not exclusively. Each volume will also include a commentary by a leading scholar or writer in the field.

SOMETHING TO BE TIPTOED AROUND

EMMA MARIE JONES

 **Grattan Street Press**

Photo Credit: Sean T. Barnes

Emma Marie Jones is an Adelaide-born poet and writer now based in Melbourne. Her short fiction, poems and essays have appeared in *Seizure, The Lifted Brow, Scum, Meanjin, Spook* and others. *Something to Be Tiptoed Around* is her first book. In 2015, the manuscript was shortlisted for the Scribe Nonfiction Prize for Young Writers, and in 2016 was longlisted for *The Lifted Brow* & RMIT non/fiction-Lab Prize for Experimental Nonfiction. Emma is a PhD candidate and teacher of Creative Writing at the University of Melbourne, and is currently working on her first novel.

Published by Grattan Street Press 2018

Grattan Street Press is the imprint of
the teaching press based in the School
of Culture and Communication at the
University of Melbourne, Parkville,
Australia.

THE UNIVERSITY OF
MELBOURNE

Grattan Street Press
School of Culture and Communication
John Medley Building,
Parkville, VIC 3010
www.grattanstreetpress.com

Printed in Australia

ISBN: 9780987625380

A catalogue record for this
book is available from the
NATIONAL
LIBRARY
OF AUSTRALIA
National Library of Australia

For Meaghan

Contents

Author Note

In 2005, when I was 17 years old, my younger sister drowned in a relative's backyard pool.

I was overseas. I flew home to meet my parents and younger brother. By the time I arrived, she had been dead for many days. Her body was already prepared for her funeral.

Last year, a Facebook friend tagged me in a photo. It was taken using one of those digital cameras that date-stamps the image, and the date showed 11 January 2005. I had never been able to remember what I had been doing the day my sister died, and now, shockingly, hidden behind a notification, here was a picture of it. I could not undo the knowing. I had been in a beer hall in Munich, sneaking beers under my schoolteacher's nose, thinking the world of myself and nothing, nothing, of my family at home.

Notes on the Genre

Sitting around a bonfire with a beer in my hand, I talk to a psychologist friend about Freud. We both think Freud, if he were alive today, would be a quack, but I think his ideas are valuable and interesting – I want to talk about Kristeva, Butler, Deleuze – and my friend thinks his ideas are positively archaic. Things utterly without value: trash. My friend is thinking, of course, about organisation – science – things that are clinical, quantitative. This is alien to me. When I'm teaching creative writing, I tell my students, 'There is no wrong answer, only your answer.' I tell them this because it is what I, as a student, was told. The making of something is qualitative, dependent entirely on its maker. Whether it is right, whether it is good, matters far less than whether it is *mine*.

When she wrote 'The Laugh of the Medusa' in 1976, Hélène Cixous was in the thick of second-wave feminism – women had been allowed access to academia for less than a century (both in France, where Cixous was located, and in Australia, where I am). In 'The Laugh of the Medusa', Cixous calls the intellectual spaces of academic writing 'a locus where the repression of women has been perpetuated, over and over, more or less consciously … where woman has never *her* turn to speak'. Now, in 2018, academia remains repressive and silencing in many of the same ways.

The crux of Cixous's argument is what brings me to genre: to fictocriticism. It is this: she is angry at men. She is angry that men in universities speak a phallocentric language they won't permit women to learn to understand. It's a language of power, and it has so many rules. It's quantitative. It's boring, it's unyielding, it has no feeling; it's based on structure and order. But what a waste! This is, writes Cixous, 'all the more serious and unpardonable in that writing is precisely *the very possibility of change*, the space that can serve as a springboard for subversive thought'.

The challenge I thus faced in theorising my grief was ironic. I wrote *Something to Be Tiptoed Around* as a Creative Writing minor thesis in 2015. In this, the year that was the tenth anniversary of my sister's death — the tenth anniversary of my being-seventeen, which was the year that I had had her and then lost her, the year of both and neither — I wanted to write about my grief. I felt that a decade was a package that could be neatly closed with prose. But what prose? Should I have wrangled my pluralised grief, my wilfully abject ideas of self and self-construction, into a phallocentric academic structure that would not, could not, hold them?

No. I wanted my voice to remain my own: I wanted my writing about grief to feel like my grief. And so I chose to move from citation to recitation, from reference and deference to performance. To a new textual space in which fiction and theory and memoir interact playfully, artfully, experimentally: fictocriticism. Defined by Anna Gibbs as a polyphonic, discordant writing – a 'haunted writing', which is to say, a writing haunted by itself – fictocriticism is a writing Gibbs says is 'traced by numerous voices', voices which work at times together and at times against one another, resulting in a text that is fluid and defiant. This fluidity and defiance often acts in direct contradiction to the authoritative conventions of traditional, quantitative academia, which dictates an existing discourse as rigid and unchanging as though it were set in stone.

The polyphony of fictocriticism results in a uniquely self-reflexive writing that embodies subjectivity and explores, textually, the relationship between author, reader and text. It is text anthropomorphised, celebrated. As Gibbs contends, fictocritical writing does not aim to *make* a point; it aims to *have* a point. It was with this in mind that I structured *Something to Be Tiptoed Around* as a physical manifestation of Bracha L. Ettinger's chaotic, pluralised matrixial gaze.

Here is how I've done it. In her introduction to Ettinger's *The Matrixial Borderspace*, Judith Butler writes about this gaze, using as its impossible object the metaphor of Eurydice. My text plays with Butler's ideas here, just as Butler plays with Ettinger's: I weave Butler's words into Jeannie's panicked, bodily brush with mortality. I am in conversation with Butler; my ideas are speaking to her ideas, and they are forced, by the coercion of the text, to speak back. Butler's words are in italics here.

> *She is presented there, and so she acquires a certain presence, but the presence does not redeem the loss, does not nullify the loss.* Cut to Jeannie looking in the mirror, touching her lip and wondering how similar this lip might be to the same lip on a living Harriet, a Harriet who would be, now, in her twenties — but no. Such reflection is dangerous, such puncturing of the prophylaxis holding back the sadness is too dangerous — cut away. *We were not supposed to look back to what may not be seen, but we did; we broke a certain law, a law that mandated that we look only and always forward to unambiguous life.* Life, Jeannie touching that lip says

to herself, what is that? *We turned around, needing to know, but it was this need, to know with certainty, that undid us. For we could not capture her that way* – the perfect nosedive – *and when we sought to have her through knowing her, we lost her.* We lost her, said the paramedics, I am sorry but we lost her, and Jeannie's mother, Well what does that mean where is she can't you find her* – *we lost her, since she cannot be had that way. But, nevertheless, it is this instant that is preserved.*

Butler's words and ideas become threads, and my words and ideas are threads, too. I am braiding them – fictocriticism is the loom on which I am braiding them – into a cloth, a rug, whatever, a story.

Later, I add more threads, the story becomes more complex. The voices of Maria Tumarkin and Julia Kristeva join Butler's and mine, and are added to the polyphony. In italics below are Butler's, Tumarkin's, and Kristeva's words, braided with mine:

Grief doesn't link across time: it tran-scends it. *A temporality in which the past is not past but is not present, in which the present emerges from a continuing, but not continuous, trauma* [Butler]. *The past enters the present as an intruder, an unwel-*

come guest; the knot tying the two togeth-
er can be loosened but will not, cannot, be
untied [Tumarkin]. Do you see? Grief is
not the aftermath of death: it is death.
It is death, infecting life [Kristeva]. It is
death, whispering in Jeannie's ear and in
mine, poking a small hole in life, in now,
and drawing our roots back, always back,
to its slow, contagious spread.

You can read more about the authors and theo-
rists whose ideas I've worked with, and see full
citations of those quotations and works, in the
Page Notes at the end of this text. I am made up
of everything I have ever touched and laid eyes
on. Most of the words in this experimental memoir are mine alone, but my grief was, is, a tangle
of all that it collided with while it was rampant,
and all that it bumps against now that it is a slow
and quiet pendulum. This hybrid thing that I have
made — regardless of whether it is good, regardless of whether it is nonsense — is *mine*. I read
more than I write: I write what I have read. And.
You know. No story is truly original. Especially not
the one about sadness.

Emma Marie Jones
2018

Foreword

I remember a swathe of hair. Always with the hair and what an easy laugh you had. People say about sisters that the one is always what the other is not. I don't know what you'd be now. Not me — obviously — but what's that? I have become unfixed. I have been defined by your absence since it started.

Were I drinking with friends now — with you — I'd uncross my legs, cross them again, an easy gesture. Toss my head and laugh, like oh, I'm such a narcissist haha. Isn't my grief so all about me. And you, being you, you'd say yes, in a whiny tone probably, or maybe you'd have grown out of whining by now. I haven't.

Do you remember when I fought you for candy and you knocked your funny bone on the furniture and fainted from the pain? I thought you were faking it. You always used to fake it. When our mother came in and saw you lying unconscious on the bedspread, saw me still punching you, I thought she'd kill me for sure.

When I remember childhood things, our brother is there and you are a ghost, present but not-present.

My brain is doing self-defence. My brain is nudging me to forget the things that tear me into pieces. It isn't fair: to lose you in real life, and in memory too. I'm angry at you sometimes. Can't you work harder, from wherever you are, to make your imprint stronger? I am trying the best that I can.

The reality I face is this. My life, and Mum's and Dad's and our brother's lives, and the lives of anyone else who has grieved or experienced trauma — they're all restructured. Life's not the onward march forward that it once was. That it perhaps was for you. It's splintered by a moment of great impact. There's a before and an after, but nothing in the after moves the same way.

Time in the after is not chronological. Events do not beget other events. Thoughts do not beget intentions. I do not treat the people I love the way that I should. I do not eat at every mealtime or sleep each night. Time is muddy, tangled, slippery. It moves sideways and across, as though your death opened a hole in the pocket time was in and it started leaking everywhere.

The after is speared by the before, but the before isn't pure like it was when we were living it. The before is contaminated by what if: a hurtful and blinding possibility that things could have gone differently. Like: what if we both had babies, and they grew up to be cousins? What if you were near to me when I had my heart broken in my twenties?

What if, when our brother and I were having drinks together with our partners in a softly lit beer garden, you were there, too – with someone, perhaps, of your own – and you were an adult, flicking a wrist under glinting lanterns, laughing about some awfully grown-up care? We'd hug goodbye at the end of the night, standing on the street, getting into separate Ubers, and you'd kiss me on each cheek, leaving a scent or a lipstick stain, but clumsily because we were neither of us ever graceful. Maybe you'd drop an earring or break a high heel as you rushed for a train, waving over your shoulder. Your laugh would still be so high-pitched, you'd snort, your nose would wrinkle and something would gather around you for a moment, the air itself taking a breath, and we'd all pause to watch you go.

And you go. But you were only three years younger than me! You were supposed to catch up. You were supposed to keep up.

SOMETHING TO BE TIPTOED AROUND

One   My Mother Once Told Me

My mother once told me – before my sister died or after? I can't remember – that she believed in ghosts. She believed in ghosts, she said, because when a person dies the energy that animated their body has to go somewhere, and it can't disperse like the ashes do when you throw them to the wind. It can't break up and redistribute itself among the blades of grass, among the small yellow flecks of acacia wattle sneaking hay fever into eyes and noses, no: energy goes bigger. It goes into the earth, the rocks, the rivers.

I believe my mother must have clung to this in the days after. That all the atoms of my sister's energy left her body and stayed together, one mass: the mass of energy that was my sister and is now a current or a breeze, now a shushing bough outside the bedroom window late at night, now a radiant beam thrown across the bedclothes in a stripe, illuminating knees and fingertips. When the earth moves – when small parts of its grand old narrative make themselves known to us – when the wind lifts the hem of her skirt, my mother closes her eyes and leans into its caress, thinking: this is her touch,

'[A]lthough mourning involves grave departures from the normal attitude to life, it never occurs to us to regard it as a pathological condition and to refer it to medical treatment. We rely on its being overcome after a certain lapse of time, and we look upon any interference with it as useless or even harmful.'

Freud, 'Mourning and Melancholia,' 243–244.

this is a message she is sending me. Because of this belief, my mother lives in a world that is dedicated to her — a world written for my mother as it happens, a world of secret, far-flung energies that belong to her grief and exist to hold it.

When you are a writer and a sore little piece of yourself breaks off and crystallises, you name it and you write a world for it and it becomes a story. This is how Jeannie comes to be. She falls, fully formed but miniature like a figurine, from the part of my consciousness where I hide my wounds so that I don't have to inspect them.

Let's say Jeannie is like me, but not enough like me that, if you met her in the supermarket or down the pub, you'd think she was me. As in physically she's similar, but not the same. Let's give her dark hair, because I've always wanted dark hair. Let's give her dark eyes because I don't have those, but let's she and I share the same small hands and wide hips and soft belly and childish flat chest that take up my space in the world because I can only write, in that sense, what I know. Let's give Jeannie the fierce will to move forward that it took me years to develop — let's give her that from the outset, as a gift.

Jeannie sees her body as a problem. This part is too lumpy, and this part too flat. This part is lopsided, and this part she hides under very baggy clothes no matter *what*. Jeannie tucks her hair behind her ears because she knows it makes her cheekbones look dramatic. Jeannie had braces for the entire duration of high school, and in the professional photo from her graduation ball, which her parents have framed on their mantelpiece, there is a big green piece of broccoli from the three-course dinner stuck in them that nobody told her about, and she will always be kind of mad about that.

Jeannie and I will share a childhood, at least partially, because it's easier that way. What that means is this: Jeannie has a younger sister whose name is Harriet, which is not the name of my sister but will do for Jeannie's, and the two sisters grew up in a big white house in the foothills where they spent their childhood afternoons climbing, barefoot and skinned-kneed, in two tall pine trees that grew at alarming acute angles to the back lawn. Jeannie remembers summer nights where she would sit in the triangle of sunlight falling through the sliding glass door, wrapping the spiral telephone cord around and around her index finger. She would swat Harriet away, the two years between them seeming vast somehow, the telephone a marker of their difference. Like one night after school: Jeannie remembers listening to the dial tone, heart drumming, as her best friend connected a secret three-way call with Jeannie's first real crush, who didn't know Jeannie was listening, and allowed him to reveal the irrevocable truth that he didn't really like her, not like that. One hand cupping the telephone's plastic mouthpiece to silence the first shaky, involuntary exhalation of heartbreak. Outside the sliding glass door, in the fading sunlight, Harriet played.

Later, when they were both teenagers, it was from Harriet that Jeannie learned what it was to be jealous of other women. Harriet had so many friends, and skin that was smooth and clear. Harriet could push out fake tears on demand and had a boyfriend. When Jeannie woke in the night, her jaw clenched tight, she would cross the hallway to Harriet's bedroom and slide under the sheets to curl beside her sister's hot, soft form as though, by osmosis, she could become more a part of her. As though what they shared was not enough.

Jeannie's sister Harriet died when Jeannie was seventeen. She drowned in a backyard pool. This is also what happened to my sister, and I am lending that story to Jeannie for a while, mostly so that I don't have to keep on carrying it by myself.

'The dead did not obey the prohibition of life on them, and they return, partial, scattered, and animated.'

Butler, 'Bracha's Eurydice,' xi.

Two Snakes

You're dropped into trauma like a small drop of hot wax into a dish of cold water. You are searing and yet you are immobilised. You're seeping fluid. You'd soften at a touch once, you'd bend and mould around whatever was in your way, but in this new surrounding you are hard and unmoving. You must be hard and unmoving because even a very small hole could cause all your insides to leak out and congeal, exposed.

Jeannie is hot wax, and I'm the one dropping her. Jeannie standing in the shadows chewing on her bottom lip. Jeannie at the airport when she heard the news. The word 'died' and some other words. Tucking her hair behind her ear like she does, saying, What?, like maybe what she really heard was 'sighed' or 'cried' or 'come outside'. If I told you about the little snakes that started growing from Jeannie's head at this point, at the dawning of her grief, would you believe me? Not snakes that you could see. Not snakes that you could braid, or that could bite you. Small ones, quiet ones, ones that only Jeannie could hear and, even then, not really know about. Snakes that whispered into infinity, snakes that were very thin and that blew around in the breeze like fine hairs.

Jeannie listens to music with lyrics about luxury and wealth, about Versace and its Medusa head. The real Medusa was made monstrous by trauma. Once a woman of great beauty, the mortal Medusa was raped by the sea god Poseidon in Athena's temple, a sacred place of wisdom. Athena, the goddess of courage, justice and strength, punished Medusa cruelly. Her long, golden hair was trans-formed into a knot of snakes, and it was made so that anybody Medusa gazed upon would be ossified: turned to stone. Lonely and raging, the product of her own sorrow, Medusa became a monster of great legend.

For this, she was beheaded by Perseus, the son of a god, and he used her head and its paralysing gaze as a weapon. Poor Medusa, without agency, robbed even of her ability to look. Her potency recognised by legend and her beauty by culture only after her head was severed — but what of her body? What of her desire? If the female gaze has the power to immobilise, is this why it must be severed from the body that commands it? Is this why it must be reduced to a trophy for a hero?

Versace's Medusa is shorn of her snakes and robbed of her potent gaze. Her severed head is locked in a circlet of keys. She is luxe, she is beautiful, she is trapped: she is everything that you desire, but she has gazed into a mirror. Hélène Cixous liberates mythical Medusa from this moment of severance: from the sunglasses and purses where she is just a cute, opulent head; from her rape and from Athena's cruel choice to punish her; from her snakes and her face, its mirror of petrification. Cixous represents her in a new space, a space where she can behave like hot wax, where she can seep and spread. She's everywhere. For Cixous, Medusa's body is endless and unsevered; it's one long thread. She and her snakes wrap around the world and time and all of us, and we don't even notice. Laughing, Medusa becomes all of us, and all of us become her. Our identities are chaotic, multiple, alterable and infinite. We pop out a new little snake whenever we feel like it. We gaze upon our sadnesses and turn them to stone. Jeannie looks to the future and she turns it to stone, and yet hurtles towards it anyway; because she must, because she will deal with it when she gets there. Green in her grief though, Jeannie doesn't know she has this power yet. She is just too new to the game.

It's like, one version of Jeannie will learn to like her snakes, and another will learn to resent them. Maybe both versions of Jeannie are small, whole

INTERVIEWER:
Tell me why Medusa is your logo.

GIANNI VERSACE:
Seduction … Sense of history, classicism. You stay with me, or no. That's it. Medusa means seduction … a dangerous attraction.

Seal, 'The Versace Moment,' 276.

Jeannies that are both parts of a bigger Jeannie, who is also whole. The words the snakes whisper live in the spaces between the wholes, and will fall into the cracks that grief made and that its after-shocks will make for the rest of Jeannie's life. For the rest of my life. Sometimes when a new crack is made, a little piece of Jeannie's insides leaks out, congeals and is exposed, but usually she's quick enough to stuff it back inside before anybody sees.

Three   The Unpalatable Sympathy of Strangers

Sadness is a process written into Jeannie's DNA, into everyone's DNA, like laughing after cumming or salivating before throwing up. It's a process awakened, unfolding for the first time, and Jeannie watches from inside of her own body with a distant interest. Her sadness is prophylactic, protecting her from itself. A thick, translucent pillow clouds her vision so that only a few images will ever remain. Like her dad, hunched sobbing over Harriet's old homework: the small neat rows of handwriting, the careful way she used to hold the pencil with her tongue poking out of her mouth – a mouth like her mum's mouth, and her mum's mouth a thin straight line now where it used to (once) be full, curving. Jeannie tucking her snakes behind her ears and watching from inside herself, deep inside. A plate of food that doesn't look like any food she's seen before. A casserole made by Mrs So-and-so, like who the fuck are all these women? They keep showing up uninvited with ceramic dishes covered in plastic wrap or faded tea towels, full of lasagnes and macaroni-somethings, even though it's 42 degrees outside, even though nobody could possibly eat.

'And the goddess turned away, and hid her eyes
Behind her shield, and, punishing the outrage
As it deserved, she changed her hair to serpents,
And even now, to frighten evil doers,
She carries on her breastplate metal vipers
To serve as awful warning of her vengeance.'

Ovid, 'Book IV,' 105.

Jeannie wonders why people throw casserole at grief like they think the casserole will smother it. Watches plate after plate of casserole pass by her untouched. The overcooked noodles and the greyish mince and peas. The unpalatable sympathy of strangers. There's no hole in her prophylactic sadness through which this food could pass. Grief isolates, quarantines. It's a demarcation by the self and of the self. A reflexive turning away, in the face of loss, from all that isn't loss itself, and so a turning in. Jeannie looks, from far away but also from very, very close up, at her deepest self. It's a duality triggered by trauma. She can't get a good picture: she can see herself whole but really distant, or close up but in tiny pieces. Alone, neither view makes sense, but she just can't put the two together.

Jeannie's mother stands behind the kitchen bench with her hands flat on its surface and says with surprise, She was only here a few days ago, preparing a peanut butter sandwich. Jeannie feels the texture of peanut butter on her tongue like glue. Sealing her mouth shut. Harriet's straight, sharp teeth puncturing the fluffy white bread! Harriet leaving the knife somewhere she shouldn't. Ants crawling on the crusts, gone hard under the air conditioning.

Somebody takes Jeannie to a restaurant. Somebody begs her to eat and she does not. A girl at school tells Jeannie that she is looking really great.

'Symptoms of melancholia include "a profoundly painful dejection, cessation of interest in the outside world, loss of the capacity to love, inhibition of all activity, and a lowering of the self-regarding feelings to a degree that finds utterances in self-reproaches and self-revilings, and culminates in a delusional expectation of punishment".'

Freud, 'Mourning and Melancholia,' 244.

Four Slime

Jeannie watches time pass on the colour of her skin. It darkens and it pales. For months, her fingers wrap around tinnies, and then they wrap around cups of tea, labels flapping on little strings. Jeannie's body is the only benchmark; the rest is a monotony that slides around her, as unresisting as water.

To melt into the big city, Jeannie gets a job at the library. She stands on the peak-hour train and, when it rounds the curve at the creek, she likes to watch all the passengers sway together like a school of fish, expressionless, unaffected by the bend. She likes the library's deep quiet and the carts of books, running her fingers down their spines, some of them untouched here in the belly of this building for months, years. Her touch perhaps longed for, missed. She turns and smells their pages; she compares them in her mind to small bodies, lodged as they are in their shelves, with their neighbours motionless, numerically ordered.

The books' small bodies speak to Jeannie in a way the human bodies of the city don't. Sometimes the closeness they have to one another in their snug, quiet shelves opens up a yearning in her own real body, and she feels a hollow heat in her cunt that throbs harder than her thoughts do. When this happens, she goes into the toilets and waits until there is nobody else in the cubicle next to her, and she humps her closed fist until the throbbing goes away.

One time, Jeannie put her hand down her pants in the Natural Sciences section, but in that moment of her vulnerability, the books changed from beautiful objects to judges, watchers, and Jeannie became afraid of them and of her own desire. She could smell herself on her fingers, and she wanted to mark those cruel paper bodies, mark them with herself so that they would acquiesce, and so that when they were carried out of the building a small part of her deepest sex would be carried too. She smeared her slime in a glossy streak along the spines. Now, she sometimes just does this whenever she gets a chance.

Jeannie shows up for work with a messy ponytail and with holes in her stockings, and nobody minds. Nobody really sees her. She is becoming very clever, my Jeannie, at not being seen. Nobody looks at you when you're in a bubble of sadness – when you could look back at them out of it with a gaze so tortured it could turn them to stone.

'I know why you haven't written. ... Because writing is at once too high, too great for you, it's reserved for the great—that is, for "great men"; and it's "silly." Besides, you've written a little, but in secret. And it wasn't good, because it was in secret, and because you punished yourself for writing, because you didn't go all the way; or because you wrote, irresistibly, as when we would masturbate in secret, not to go further, but to attenuate the tension a bit, just enough to take the edge off.'

Cixous, 'Laugh of the Medusa,' 876–877.

Five   The Perfect Nosedive

There's this flower stand on Swanston Street that Jeannie has to pass on her way to the library. She hates it. The flower stand is small and painted an inoffensive shade of forest green, and it sells bunches of red roses priced by the rose. She hates those too. She hates the death-row succulents in their glass mason jars, waiting to be chosen and taken, with pitiful optimism, to a sunless office cubicle. She watches those succulents, fat and prickly and tubular, trying to photosynthesise as much as they can before that happens. She wonders if they know they are going to die.

Mostly, though, Jeannie hates the flower stand because of the lilies. Because of the lilies, the flower stand is spectral, terrible. It is a small point in the fabric of time and space that proves to her that this fabric is not linear, no: it's folded in upon itself, and the flower stand is a pin that, when Jeannie passes it, pokes a little hole right through now and into her parents' living room ten years ago. The smell of lilies reminds Jeannie that grief is elastic. When she smells those flowers, sees their white waxy cones and the tall bright stamens poking rudely out of them — like they don't care how sad you are, they are going to be so beautiful anyway — when Jeannie walks by those lilies, she is transported right back to that first bloom of her anguish, when it was fresh.

Memory's a funny thing. Let's try something, just you and me. An experiment: think of a moment that you loved, a special one. Steeped in emotion. (I'll tell you that the moment I'm thinking of is one from not very long ago, when somebody took my hand under a table in a restaurant, all candlelight flicker and wineglass clink, and said to me, too hot-faced to meet my eyes: you are my favourite person.)

Think of that moment and then think of all the other times you have thought of that moment. At all of those times, you have added an extra layer to that moment, a filter, a wrapper, a trace. You have done this and done this and done this, until the moment itself is gone, lost, but you won't grieve it — it's better this way, improved. It stirs something hard and light and wonderful in your tummy. It's drenched in *you* — but it's a thing entirely its own. It's one moment that is connected to all the other moments that you brought it into, all by yourself, and when you think about it you connect them all together and you light them up, a constellation.

That's memory. Grief doesn't do that. Grief doesn't link across time: it transcends it. A temporality in which the past is not past but is not present, in which the present emerges from a continuing, but not continuous, trauma. The past enters the present as an intruder, an unwelcome guest; the knot tying the two together can be loosened but will not, cannot, be untied. Do you see? Grief is not the aftermath of death: it is death. It is death, infecting life. It is death, whispering in Jeannie's ear and in mine, poking a small hole in life, in now, and drawing our roots back, always back, to its slow, contagious spread.

The small hole works like this: there's a sphere, right in the centre of Jeannie's vision, in which her parents' living room ten years ago hangs like a Christmas decoration. The sphere bends Jeannie's parents' living room like a fish-eye lens. What is bending Jeannie's parents' living room is maybe time, or maybe the pressure of memory, or maybe the deadweight of grief. Whatever has bent it has also distorted it, misrepresented it: the curtains that Jeannie knows were blue ten years ago are, in the sphere, kind of purple; the fake Persian rug under the coffee table had a stain on it where Harriet vomited one time, and the stain is bigger

'[T]he trace, the sign of loss, the remnant of loss, is understood as the link, the occasional and nearly impossible connection, between trauma and beauty itself.'

Butler, 'Bracha's Eurydice,' xii.

than it really was, more vivid, a visual klaxon, all plaintive, like look at me, here, I'm here.

And Jeannie looks at it. She tilts forward into it, a perfect nosedive. Her body arcs into it, and all the grey morning people on Swanston Street with their hands in their coat pockets turn to stare at the space on the footpath where the girl was and now isn't, and Jeannie is following the trace. The trace, the sign of loss, the remnant of loss, the link: the occasional and nearly impossible connection between trauma and beauty itself. The trace is fragile, a filament, a yellow brick road that Jeannie can follow, if she doesn't break it, between spheres. In her parents' living room now hangs Swanston Street, an orb in which the people move about in miniature. Jeannie watches them for a while, watches a tiny tram move slowly, like a toy, before she turns. The rug! The sliding glass door, through which she had watched Harriet, so many times, use her body like it was a durable thing! The trace is the fleeting image: it pulls on memory, an instant of remembering that vanishes upon remembering. To articulate it is to lose it. Harriet — oh, Harriet! Jeannie's little heart is keening now for her in the spherical living room all warped and wrongly coloured — to articulate her is to lose her. Her lush, sunny face appears in

Jeannie's mind, a flash of an image that's perfect, for a moment, and then trembles and then shifts, post-impressionistic. Freckles appear where they weren't. Or were they — now which side of her face did the smile quirk up on, which eye was smaller than the other, Jeannie can't remember anymore, and it's this desperate clawing at memory that undoes memory, it's this picking at the scab that opens the wound.

She is presented there, and so she acquires a certain presence, but the presence does not redeem the loss, does not nullify the loss. Cut to Jeannie looking in the mirror, touching her lip and wondering how similar this lip might be to the same lip on a living Harriet, a Harriet who would be, now, in her twenties — but no. Such reflection is dangerous, such puncturing of the prophylaxis holding back the sadness is too dangerous — cut away. We were not supposed to look back to what may not be seen, but we did; we broke a certain law, a law that mandated that we look only and always forward to unambiguous life. Life, Jeannie touching that lip says to herself, what is that? We turned around, needing to know, but it was this need, to know with certainty, that undid us. For we could not capture her that way — the perfect nosedive — and when we sought to have her through knowing her, we lost

'[W]e will not lose her for the first time, but we will lose her again, and it will be by virtue of our own gaze...'

Butler, 'Bracha's Eurydice,' viii.

her. We lost her, said the paramedics, I am sorry but we lost her, and Jeannie's mother, Well what does that mean where is she can't you find her — we lost her, since she cannot be had that way. But, nevertheless, it is this instant that is preserved.

It is this instant that is preserved.

Jeannie's parents' living room ten years ago is wobbling in her vision. The thick, translucent pillow of her sadness — how much she has held inside herself, and for so long! Bouquets of lilies cover every surface of the room, and Jeannie remembers the heatwave, the smell. The rotting flowers falling on the living room tiles and the broomstick becoming tangled with their soft, damp parts.

Jeannie sits back onto a sofa that isn't really there, and sees Harriet's face melting like an acid trip, eyes rolled back in her head, just the whites showing, splitting open so that the tall bright stamens can tear through and grow, upright, erect —

And Jeannie's lying on the footpath, and someone — someone in an apron full of thorny clippings from the stems of roses priced by the rose — is leaning over her and saying, Are you okay?

And all the people with their hands in their coat pockets are staring with something that could be concern or embarrassment or disapproval, and

Jeannie, standing, brushing her knees where the stockings are torn and where blood is coming out. *We lost her*. Jeannie says, Yes, I'm okay, and puts her head right down and walks onward, to the library, to work.

'He, enamoured, fearing lest she should flag, and impatient to behold her, turned his eyes; and immediately she sank back again.'

Ovid, 'Book X', 47–75.

Six   A Butcher's or a Cosmetologist's

When she steps into the air-conditioned foyer of the funeral home, Jeannie feels like she's stepping outside of her body and entering hyperspace. There is a sensation that her limbs are growing very long and multiplying and wiggling in all directions, like they're turning into spaghetti. She watches this with fascination, but at the same time she can't see it happening.

The walls in the viewing room are the same peach-pink as the carpet: it's a colour Jeannie associates with surgeries she's seen on television. The coffin, perhaps white or perhaps not, has a lid in two parts. The bottom part is closed over Harriet's feet, and the top part is open, revealing her face and torso. Inside, it's lined with something silky. Harriet is wearing clothes that Jeannie can tell their mother chose carefully. She wants to touch them, but they already feel like artefacts. The shirt is one that Jeannie borrowed often; she drank her first beer while wearing it last. It will be cremated, along with the rest of Harriet. The shirt that Jeannie wore the first time she drank a beer will soon be ash.

When we see death and its accessories, something happens. It prompts a delineation of self, a small and silent and subconscious SOS signal, a setting of coordinates, a mapping and positioning of the self, a quiet motion that could be for comfort or survival. When we are confronted with death in this way – looking at it, really looking at *it* itself, its physical manifestation – our own physical selves are positioned on the very border of their statuses as living beings. Our minds recoil so violently and so decisively from such borders that they create little chambers within themselves to house such horrors. These new spaces are borderspaces. They're liminal, they are in flux.

The chamber my mind created to hold my horror was this peach-pink funeral home. There was a need, perhaps – when my brain demarcated its territory of aliveness without telling me it was demarcating anything at all – there was a need for me, in this moment of nearness to death, to tether myself to something that was soft and pink and warm.

This is one possibility. Another possibility is that I, as author, am deliberately misremembering the funeral home so that I can make it as monstrous and abject as possible. Drenching its recirculated air in formaldehyde, and masking that smell with

'At traumascapes, the knot tying the present and the past together often cannot be untied.'

Tumarkin, *Traumascapes*, 14.

the sweeter and yet more suffocating one of lilies. (Does it matter which Jeannie will smell first? They both smell, to me and to her, of death.) Paint its walls the colour of offal and the carpets to match. The funeral home is an abject space. Is it a butcher's or a cosmetologist's? Is it a place to grieve or a place to sicken? It's absolutely either, or both. It's a physical checkpoint between the world of the living and the world of the dead.

Harriet's eyes are closed but she doesn't look like she is sleeping. (Harriet would sleep with her limbs spread out like a jumping jack, her head on one side, hair plastered to her bright, dewy cheek. Jeannie remembers her like this, with a little string of spit vibrating in the corner of her open mouth with each breath.) In her coffin, Harriet is still, but she is not relaxed. She's colourless and, when Jeannie notices this, the room's peach glow makes sense, reflecting as it does off the blue-white skin so that it almost looks like there might be blood in Harriet's veins, a blush in Harriet's cheeks.

Jeannie is glad that the bottom part of the lid is closed over Harriet's hands, because abruptly she is terrified to see what they would look like, knotted into a staged position of repose by another pair of hands, a stranger's hands. Harriet's hair is brushed neatly, and Jeannie longs to mess it up because Harriet never brushed her hair, never, not even for school photos, and it looks weird, Harriet's mouth looks weird without its little corner flick like it's about to either smile or open up and say something — Harriet never could keep still — and the peach walls of the room are way too thick, and Jeannie knows her face is pinched and long. She can feel her mouth going lower than it normally goes, feel it going right down to the bottom of her chin and still dropping.

Seven   A Hall of Mirrors

Jeannie wonders, curled up in her single bed in the summer weeks after Harriet's funeral, whether it is possible to become allergic to a word. A word that was applied to you, a word that has expired from you. Jeannie pushes with her mind, wondering whether it's possible to remove this word like clothing. The word 'sister'. That double-ended word: to be and to have. Jeannie is tired of traipsing 'sister' behind her like a veil. She's tired of dropping the word like a heavy stone into a still pool of sad faces, rippling their comfort; she is tired of having it offered to her, gently but relentlessly, like needles in a hospital.

Beyond guilt, beyond sadness, Jeannie seeks herself, seeks to know herself in relation to the absence of 'sister'. This absence opens a hole in language. There is a hole in language, and Jeannie's snakes are filling it with whispers, shifting the borders of who she is. Pushing those borders inwards but also outwards, realigning her small orbit, tightening it or maybe expanding it so that she will see more of herself or more of everything else.

'The ferryman drove him away
entreating, and, in vain, desiring
again to cross *the stream*.'

Ovid, 'Book X', 47–75.

'[T]he wonder of being several—she doesn't defend herself against these unknown women whom she's surprised at becoming, but derives pleasure from this gift of alterability.'

Cixous, 'Laugh of the Medusa,' 889.

When his beautiful girlfriend Eurydice died, heroic Orpheus went into the underworld to get her out. Hades, the god of the underworld, gave Orpheus one shot. If you can find your girlfriend, you can have her, he said. I won't give you any help. Lead her home, he said, and she's all yours. But you can't look back to check that she's following you. You have to trust her. This was Hades's ultimatum. You have to trust her. If you turn around to look, I'll keep her here forever.

Of course, Orpheus looked back. How could anyone not look? Even when you know it will cost you: all that your instincts tell you, all the time, is to look back. Jeannie knows this; Jeannie is right there in that moment.

Jeannie, like Orpheus, is looking back, back towards the one thing that can't be looked back upon. Even as she sheds it, the label 'sister' is the threshold between what was and what will be. Sister Jeannie between life and death. Sister Jeannie between a living, breathing Harriet and a ghostly Harriet, a Eurydice-Harriet, a Harriet who vanishes in the instant you look at her. And so Jeannie looks at her, at this spectral Harriet who cannot be looked back upon, with a gaze like Medusa's: immobilising, destructive, an instrument of desire that is also a weapon, a curse. She looks at Harriet and, in her grief, she seeks desperately to turn to stone even this final instant of her vanishing. Locked forever in this fleeting encounter, Jeannie is Orpheus, looking back; at the same time, Jeannie is Medusa, petrifying the moment of Harriet's disappearance, memorialising the moment in which she is lost forever.

I wonder: is Eurydice sad because she's beautiful, or is she beautiful because she's sad? Sadness and beauty and femininity are by now a kind of triad that Jeannie is learning to situate herself within to her advantage. With her slackening veil of sisterhood wrapped around her face, or trailing loose from her like she is an Ophelia floating sadly down a river. With her snakes, and stone eyes all powerful and hard. Jeannie can be inside the trinity or outside of it, or both at the same time. Whatever makes things work for her. She can sit on the brink.

Eurydice was bitten on her little foot by a viper and that's how she died. Jeannie wonders whether one of her vipers will bite her and whether she'd die if it did. Can you be poisoned by your own venom? Can you make yourself sick enough to pass into another world, an underworld where souls swim and moan forever, lost? She wonders if anybody would come to search for her in the

'[Eurydice's] image is redoubled, and there seems to be a set of them, all of them fading and appearing at once.'

Butler, 'Bracha's Eurydice,' viii.

underworld, if she'd have an Orpheus of her very own who'd lead her back to the world of the living. Whether they'd be in love with her, whether they'd be cute. Whether they'd turn around to see if she was following behind. Jeannie, sitting on the brink, wonders: would she follow? Her feet are so tired already from all the walking she has done, just to get to where she is; just to get away from where she was.

Jeannie doesn't know it yet, but this is why I made her. To do what I can't do: to pass between worlds. My own little ghost, my own fractal-mirror self, whole and fully formed, and yet just a small part of something else, something bigger. A small part whose entire world is grief; whose entire experience is slipping into the underworld to seek what is lost, and then resurfacing to the realm of the living to admit defeat. My own poor little Orpheus, lost forever between two worlds but insubstantial enough, borderline enough, to exist in both. Searching for something she'll inevitably, upon finding it, surrender.

And so: the looking back captures. It possesses and destroys. The instant of Eurydice's disappearance fights, though, against this destruction in a way that must always win simply because, to its enemy, it is incomprehensible. An ossified tangle.

Fleeting and permanent, a gaze that happens once forever, and over and over again in a new measure of time. Eternalised and internalised, vain and self-reflexive, narcissistic, grieving and self-destructive, pluralising, fracturing, transcending all recognition. Meeting at this shared pin on the map, Jeannie and Medusa, Harriet and Eurydice are mimetic, braided, fused. They carry each other's burdens, they unify each other's myths. The encounter that they're locked in and its process of becoming cancel out the power of the unwanted, ordered gaze that would reject and destroy them. Jeannie and her snakes, Jeannie and her stony gaze will search forever — the snakes with their tongues out, tasting the air — and when they find her, when they find Harriet, her ghostly footsteps will be silent in the darkness, and she will follow blindly. They will seep into one another, trying to be more of each other than they already are: they're an unbeatable team. But Jeannie — Jeannie will surely turn.

In her turning, Jeannie triggers contradiction, just as Orpheus triggered it before her. When Eurydice is looked at, she ceases to be — and yet, in the moment she's looked at, she's corporeal, apprehensible. She is present and she's gone, both at the same time. In the instant of her vanishing, she's plural, contradictory. As in a hall of mirrors, her image is redoubled, and there seems to be a set of them, all of them fading and appearing at once. The image of Eurydice echoes: intangible, unreal. She is the object of Orpheus's gaze, but she can't ever really *be* an object. She cannot be possessed. She cannot be looked at. She cannot be invoked or defined. She becomes infinite, and she transcends and spans: like Cixous's Medusa, Eurydice passes into infinity and becomes several. She retreats into her underworld, swimming with the souls who moan, and perhaps she joins them, and perhaps she misses her boyfriend Orpheus, and perhaps she's glad he's gone, and we will never know because the stories we are told did not write her voice.

And all of this awaits poor Jeannie, who does not yet know that the hole in language, opened by loss, will never be filled. That one word – 'sister', a clean word, a normal word – will have a little extra weight in it, a kind of sag in the chest whenever it is written or spoken, heard or read, for the rest of Jeannie's life.

Eight   All the Holes

At the bar at the top of the hill in an hour, Jeannie will meet a painter from Tinder who will, later, remove all of her clothes and graze each bone of her ribcage with his teeth, and fuck her slowly and then quickly and then selfishly. In the morning, with one hand on the front gate, he will make a promise to call her and then break that promise and her heart, which has been broken many times before in these small ways, enough times that this break will be invisible, unnoticeable, will mend slowly but quietly and on its own. But all of this is later, in an hour and tomorrow. Right now Jeannie and her body are bending forward to pull up stockings, bending right and left to dab perfume on knobs of wrists. Jeannie and her body are squatting by the mirror to apply, carefully, a face.

This face is first a paste and then a powder, applied with the heels of her hands and then a small round sponge. A brown stripe under the cheekbones for dramatic shadow, a pink one on the apples for glow, a white one on the planes for highlights, so that her face is like a tub of neapolitan ice cream until she blends it with a big angled

'[S]he goes and passes into infinity.'

Cixous, 'Laugh of the Medusa,' 889.

brush. Harriet used to eat the strawberry stripe straight from the tub and leave the chocolate and vanilla, which Jeannie would remember if I let her, but I spare her the little stab.

In the background plays an empowering pop playlist about a) being desired and b) transcending desire. Jeannie dances to it but with the volume down, because she doesn't want her housemates to hear. She is embarrassed about needing songs like these to feel sexy. Her limbs move in ways they never move in clubs or at parties. Whenever she is in public, her body becomes so stiff and cumbersome.

Jeannie pouts into the mirror and paints her lips a shade of pink that matches her nipples exactly. She does this because she knows that men like to think about fucking all the time, even subconsciously, while they are listening to women speak, while they are watching women's mouths speak.

When you're lonely! When you're lonely like Jeannie, when your self-worth doesn't exist inside yourself but is generated externally, is generated inside guys like this guy, guys who smell good and paint badly and own expensive sneakers; when the world is warped by your sadness, when your snakes whisper things into your ear like, fuck him, do it, he's too cool for you anyway — well, let's not make excuses for Jeannie. She knows what she's doing, or more like she knows she doesn't know what she's doing but she's doing it anyway. We've all been there.

Subconsciously, Jeannie knows that men from Tinder have this preconceived notion of what femininity is supposed to look like, so she's applying it to her body like a suit of armour. She knows about the face she has to wear, about the fetishisation of sadness and hipbones, the anxious pallor of the mourner. Knows that these things might qualify her to be someone's muse for a night or a week before they become bored. There is no being behind doing, effecting, becoming – but femininity is not that cut and dried, and neither is the version of a cute girl Jeannie's dressing up as right now as though it's a Halloween costume. It feels to Jeannie like an uncomfortable skin: her painted sex mouth, her snakes pinned restlessly up on top of her head and resenting the restriction, her inward-turned self forced outward, forced now to be the object of a hungry and licentious gaze.

At the bar at the top of the hill, the painter is in the beer garden, rolling cigarettes for the both of them with his very long fingers – fingers that, when Jeannie looks at them, she can't help but imagine two of in her cunt a little later. And she knows that he can see her looking at his fingers in this way, and she knows that he mistakes her lonely need to be filled – her need to have all the holes in her self and in her body filled with solid things – for lust, and that he likes this. Still, she will let him fuck her just to feel something, anything. He licks his lips before he puts the cigarette between them.

But the body is just language, and the thing that will forever stunt its flight into freedom and infinity is our abiding instinct to identify and name it. To the painter, Jeannie's reduced to her fucked-up pantomime: a vacant body, a painted, panting doll. Turning inward on herself as she does, Jeannie wins her body back by shedding it: by outgrowing language, by leaving it behind; by pluralising her self and the meaning of her self over and over again. Doing this, Jeannie rejects the self-imposed order inherent in concepts of identity and recognition and individuation, she rejects the assumption that she's distinct, that she's one thing or another thing, and that she must be recognised that way. Shunning signifiers, ceasing to place meaning inside them and so stripping them of worth, killing them, laying them waste, Jeannie transcends semiotics, becomes fluid, several, infinite. In her grief, Jeannie is liberated from meaning and hierarchy. Shedding not identifiers but language, language itself – the liberation! – Jeannie's body fades. I mean, if the body's just language and the whole world only meaning, then the body is unfinished, incomplete. It's flickering in and out of view, and we do know how Jeannie likes to remain unseen.

She watches, fading into her puffy coat, while this guy licks his lips before he puts his cigarette between them. She watches him with slow eyes like a cat's, and he says, Wait, where did you go?

'There is no gender identity
behind the expressions
of gender; that identity is
performatively constituted by
the very "expressions" that are
said to be its results.'

Butler, *Gender Trouble*, 25.

Nine   Something to Be Tiptoed Around Until It
Goes Away

Harriet died in the summertime, lurid blue lino-
leum lining the backyard pool: a tomb. Jeannie
wasn't there, in the backyard, when it happened —
when Harriet's lungs filled up with the chlorinated
water, when her little body floated to the top and
somebody cried out, Hey Harriet are you — Jeannie
wasn't there. When Jeannie tries to remember the
days that came afterward, all she gets is a formless
lump that, when she pokes it, spews out tiny pieces without syntax, tiny pieces of a day or a night or
a week — internal, trembling, timeless terrors.

The sun a ruthless watcher, Jeannie spends the
summer in her bedroom. Jeannie and her jellyfish
heart. The ghost of Harriet sitting where Harriet used
to sit, perched on the end of the bed, crouched
on the windowsill, bugging Jeannie for a book or a
lip gloss or a favourite CD. Jeannie knows she can
go into Harriet's bedroom now and take all the lip
glosses and CDs she wants, and she does go in there,
but she doesn't touch anything. When she walks
the route from the door to the bed, she treads quietly so her footsteps don't disturb the carpet where
Harriet's small, bare feet once would tread.

Are we all just meat, or are we just the floating energy housed within it? Jeannie sits underneath the air-conditioning vent, and her snakes sway in its fabricated breeze. She wonders if grief is chronic. She wonders if her grief will stretch to make room for her as she grows, or if it will envelop her and, if it does, will it be sweet or terrible. She wonders whether grief becomes a landmark in your life that you refer to like a stone on the horizon, or if it is something that diminishes, something to be tiptoed around until it goes away.

'It is really only because
we know so well how to
explain [mourning] that this
attitude does not seem to us
pathological.'

Freud, 'Mourning and Melancholia,' 244.

Ten Not All Ghosts Are of Living Things

Have you ever stood on a train and watched your reflection in the window as the carriage slides up to the platform and comes to rest there? Let's say that on this platform is a person standing, waiting parallel to you so that your faces line right up, staring at their own reflection in the window when the train stops. This person is seeing through their reflection to your face, and you are looking out through your reflection to their face. For just one moment, your eyes press on each other — you speak through this pressure — you both say, with your eyes, something kind of like: I see you, I see you, I see myself in you. Over this stranger's face is mirrored the most familiar face of all, your face, your own face, and this makes that stranger's face the most loving and wonderful face you have ever seen. A mask, a ghost. And this person both knows and does not know that they are wearing, for this fleeting moment, your face. They know and do not know that they have slipped through a train window and into your skin. They wear it for a moment and then they move, or the train does, and you have your face back, all to yourself, none the worse for wear. Not all ghosts are of living things.

We can slide into the guises of one another in this way, like trains pulling into the station. Arriving at our destinations. We can try one another on for size, briefly, through the glass buffer. Our selves interact, reflect, but never truly touch. Even as I drop my hot wax figurine Jeannie into the textual underworld I've created for her – no, created her for, whatever – even as I expel her in an act of revulsion, a discharge of the part of myself that's grieving and can only exist outside of the parts of myself that aren't, I envy Jeannie her freedom, her fluidity. She and her snakes can inhabit the spaces I have written for them in a way that I can never fully inhabit my own body, my own world. That's the ironic part of having broken myself into two: the abjection of my grief has liberated me, but only part of me. Only Jeannie.

Me and Jeannie, Jeannie and me: our reflexive, shattered selfhood is a fleeting encounter occurring at a shared borderspace, a train at the platform: the platform the thin line between life and death, between text and world. Our eyes press upon each other – my eyes and Jeannie's eyes, Medusa's eyes and Orpheus's eyes. There is a familiar face mirrored over a stranger's face: a spectre who cannot be looked upon immobilised, turned in her dying moment into a statue of my mourning.

My sister, a teenage girl forever now, would slam her bedroom door to cry behind it. More than ten years after she died, I watched my mother's eyes flick when the wind pushed a door abruptly closed.

Maybe the kinetic processes of my sister's body — a breath, a blink, a heartbeat — have fallen away from the ash of her and scattered, now; maybe they brush against me in new ways. Maybe it is my sister, or the concept of her and her loss, tearing Jeannie apart from me and animating her. If you believed in ghosts you would say that this was an act of kindness. But in my hands I hold objects my sister would never have believed possible; for her sake and my own, I imagine that my eyes are my sister's long-dead eyes, a live stream to the underworld.

If my mother's world is full of secret messages from ghosts — a world in which every unknown force is a gesture, a touch — my world is the reverse. Every action is a performance, a missive to an audience of one. Both of our grief-worlds keep my sister at the centre of all things — a pole around which our lives will spin until they end — and yet collapse her into our selves, so that she has become my mother

'She, hapless one! both
stretching out her arms and
struggling to be grasped, and to
grasp him, caught nothing but
the fleeting air.'

Ovid, 'Book X', 47–75.

and she has become me, she has become Harriet and, too, Jeannie. All of us so similar, separated by the glass, unable to see or reach the other through it. And my sister – perhaps she watches, but probably she doesn't. Probably she can't.

Within Jeannie in this way – and so, within me – the gaze through the glass is a long, thick, glowing rope, and it binds the self and the other together by the eyeballs. The self and the other are two fragments of one whole: two partial, shattered pieces that are never really joined together but never really broken quite apart. And they are, or can be, me and Jeannie, and they are, or can be, Eurydice and Medusa – yeah, picture this – they're the women of the myths! The women who were given gazes, as weapons or as death sentences, by the gods for whom they were playthings. They are, or can be, Eurydice and Medusa, and they are, or can be, me and Jeannie, and so it occurs again, or must occur. The prophylaxis must collapse: at some point, I must look Jeannie in the eye and tell her who she is.

In the underworld, Jeannie carries the burden of my trauma for me, she bears witness to my trauma. The gaze touches: it's a way, the only way, to touch, to try to touch. It's the closest I can come to Jeannie, to press my face right up against the glass and try to call to her, try to reach her, Jeannie –

Jeannie doesn't know it yet, and maybe she never will. So busy painting on her sex mouth while she's waiting for the train that she can't see through the glass she's looking into, can't see through her own reflection to her creator's face behind it. She doesn't know because she doesn't want to know that she exists to be my proxy, my envoy, a witness to my anguish and my grief. She wallows in memory because she doesn't want to face the duty I have crafted her to fulfil: to carry me to the Orphean underworld and to swim us through it, to search for Harriet, which isn't the name of my sister but will do for Jeannie's. To do the unthinkable: to turn, flipping her snakes like glossy hair in a shampoo commercial, and throw her ossifying gaze upon the ghostly Harriet, treading so quietly behind her. No — to realise, in this moment of destruction, that what she's searching for cannot be Harriet at all, but must be, can only be a shadow of herself. Harriet is gone, lost forever. She has passed over that threshold into death and all that is left of her is the trace, the remnant of loss — but all of this is memory, and all of this is within the self. Not part of Harriet, but part of Jeannie. Part of me, of me, on this side of the glass and on that side. This side and the other side.

'[W]hen I am under the gaze of the Other, beheld by the desire of the Other, *I/non-I* am ... an ensemble that multifocuses the gaze, while being pluralised by it.'

Ettinger, *The Matrixial Borderspace*, 87.

Harriet! You who sang in the shower and slid notes under my bedroom door. Harriet! With your bitten nails and scabby knees. Harriet! Harriet! This is what we truly grieve. Me and Jeannie, sitting on either side of the glass, so far apart that we cannot see each other. This is what we grieve. This loss of you, Harriet, irrevocable. This loss of you, and our split, shared self's endless reproduction of this loss: endless, endless. Our Orphean search, through text and self: traces, remnants and links of memory slipping away as we tug at the thread; warping, distorting, sliding like a train from the platform just as we turn and begin to see the image behind the glass.

'[I]n this kind of remembering, an act of remembering calls for a partial reliving of an unassimilated past.'

Tumarkin, *Traumascapes*, 12.

'Beauty will no longer be forbidden.'

Cixous, 'Laugh of the Medusa,' 876.

Eleven   Aqua Profonda

When the cloudy lid lifts from the city in early
October, the sun bears down with great focus and
it softens Jeannie's bones until she hangs limp in
her hot skin. Here is Jeannie's body, disembodied,
laid out on a towel on the hot cement. As you see
her, she is lovely. Not the loveliest, just another
woman by the pool. Another wet dark hair pink
limb tangle, you know the kind: big sunglasses and
the little fingers worrying the swimsuit where it
rides up on the butt, hoping nobody will notice,
but of course you do, of course you do. She is what
you have been searching for, and you have found
her, and yet in this moment of finding her you will
witness her in some way disappear.

And this is how she does it. Unravelling on the
inside, her body watching itself disembowel itself
mmm-hmm, flesh twisting inside out, but on
the inside out only more flesh still to twist. This
restless knot of grief that she must carry. This restless trembling weight. But will it float? The body
on the inside wishing to be waterproof. Flinching
away from the splashing and the simple beauty
of the sunlight on the chlorine blue. Every droplet

shrapnel. The famous sign an augury, a hidden secret portent. *DANGER DEEP WATER — AQUA PROFONDA*. Profound danger, yeah. The twisting aching flesh. But Melbourne heat's a syrup that you find yourself suspended in for months at a time — it yellows your vision — the wet footprints on the cement evaporate as you watch them. They disappear like ghosts. Jeannie standing now, extending one leg, one toe, towards the surface and her inner body shrieking don't you dare — don't you dare —

Ah! She drops into the water like a pin. My Jeannie! Just the way I dropped her into this world. Straight into twenty-seven. Jeannie with a gradu-ate mind and a gradual heart. Jeannie with a sex mouth, Jeannie with a smudged cheek. Jeannie swimming freestyle with a perfect stroke, good girl. I always knew she would be so buoyant when the time came. Jeannie, Jeannie! Jeannie, how I love you! Jeannie, I made you and you are me and mine. And yet how cruelly I have caged you! How selfishly I weighed you down. How sadistically I wrote you into being, full of hope, only to suffer and suffer again!

Water, so perfectly liminal, dilutes things, dis-solves things. It can kill you, you can float on it, you can move through it, weightless and powerful

'Write your self. Your body must be heard. Only then will the immense resources of the unconscious spring forth.'

Cixous, 'Laugh of the Medusa,' 880.

and smooth. Suspended amniotic in this way, Jeannie's on the border. Jeannie's neither conscious nor unconscious, neither living nor dead, neither fully textual nor fully realised, always one toe in the pool and one toe on the hot cement. She cannot live among us in our ordered world; ejected and dejected, she must write her own, but she is me so I must write it for her. As Jeannie rules this desolate territory, so must I rule it, too – with her, through her, as her. And what I've written her is grief, only grief. I don't give her joy or love or friendship, pleasure or anticipation. Jeannie doesn't get to dance in a basement club to 'I'm a Slave 4 U'; she doesn't get to wake up on a windy morning to a soft, sleepyheaded kiss. Jeannie has never had her passport stamped, or tenderly potted a seedling, or taken a mirror selfie after a new haircut. She'll never know these things because I keep them for myself. Jeannie doesn't feel the water of the pool sliding past her body, cool, receptive: only pushes through it dutifully, knowing that she must. One lap and then another lap. She doesn't see the beauty I surround her with; looking at it, she turns it wastefully to stone.

Thrust into this self-mirroring landscape to seek what we – what I – have lost, Jeannie must be deprived of satisfaction, of distraction. Why else would she continue on her quest? The underworld of grief is swirling both around her and within her, and somewhere, somewhere there is Harriet, which isn't the name of my sister but will do for Jeannie's. The abject horror of grief is the danger deep water she must swim through, and I will write Jeannie through it, one lap and then another lap, until we find her.

This world of Jeannie's is, after all, only text, and text is a medium we swim through, a medium we put things in hoping that they will be buoyant enough to make sense all on their own. One lap and then another lap. Jeannie never stops marking off the boundaries of her universe, but I'm always moving them. They're unknowable and fluid – grief is fracturing, shifting, dancing like the sunlight on the surface of the chlorine blue. I mean, Jeannie's just a piece of my self that I've written, but at what point does she spin into collision with the real? At what point do I tuck my own hair behind my own ears, my real ears in this real world, and feel a small snake sprouting from the soft skin there? At what point do I look into the mirror and see Jeannie's sad eyes looking back at me, her dark eyes where my green ones once were — see her, redoubled, a thousand Jeannies fading and appearing all at once? When your whole world, and your whole existence in it, is defined by something fractured, you must constantly question your solidity. You must quiver like a distant object in a heatwave, you must fluctuate. You must watch your shadow evaporate like a wet footprint on the hot cement.

'The future must no longer be determined by the past. I do not deny that the effects of the past are still with us. But I refuse to strengthen them by repeating them, to confer upon them an irremovability the equivalent of destiny.'

Cixous, 'Laugh of the Medusa,' 875.

Autobiography as Enacted Theory

Emma Marie Jones's *Something to Be Tiptoed Around* is experimental autobiography. A presentation of the self, experimentally. A self, experimented on. The self here is literally externalised in the character of Jeannie: a blasted self, a blighted Other, 'poor Jeannie', who must bear it all, when our author/ narrator cannot. The duality of the self is triggered by trauma, in this case the early, tragic death of a sibling: 'This is also what happened to my sister, and I am lending that story to Jeannie for a while, mostly so that I don't have to keep on carrying it by myself.' And later: '[Jeannie] and her snakes can inhabit the spaces I have written for them in a way that I can never fully inhabit my own body, my own world.' One of the work's key claims is that neither subjectivity nor grief can be *ordered*, and Jeannie is the figure forced, violently, into the underworlds of both. The braiding of the always-elsewhere posi-tion of woman with the always-elsewhere position of the grieving self is enacted with exceptional suc-cess throughout this work.

Something to Be Tiptoed Around presents enact-ed theory. It absorbs rather than converses with its key points of reference by Cixous, Kristeva, Butler, Ettinger, Lacan, Freud. Hélène Cixous's urgent rhythms and her call to action abound throughout the work ('Listen: when we are confronted with death in this way, something happens'), as, of course, does her imagery in Jeannie as the snake-headed, immobilising Medusa, after Cixous's famous essay 'The Laugh of the Medusa'. Cixous's is one of those perennial voices: her *écriture féminine,* though over forty years old now as a concept, retains its currency, its exigency. The chaotic, matrixial and autocritical nature of Jones's work, after Cixous's, with its textual play, repetition, recitation and experimentation, aims to disrupt linguistic binary. The self-conscious use of quotations becomes the object of the book's gentle derision, while simultaneously incorporated into its own cadence: citing 'academic-speak' for its poetry rather than its authority. Each small creative decision like this reinforces the work's overarching claim, from Gibbs: that autocritical or experimental writing is not making but *having* a point. It is itself, as an artistic and critical form, its own argument. Perhaps the most well-known recent example of auto-theory is Maggie Nelson's *The Argonauts*, a surprise bestseller that explores Nelson's relationship with her transgender partner and their children through the lens of the history of gender theory. Like Nelson's book, and other works of auto-theory, *Something to Be Tiptoed Around* challenges the conventional erasure of the body and personhood of the theorist.

The disruption of the formal, traditional binary between autobiography and theory is mirrored in Jones's challenge to the binary between self and other. In 'Not All Ghosts Are of Living Things', we read:

> The self and the other are two fragments of one whole: two partial, shattered pieces that are never really joined together but never really broken quite apart. And they are, or can be, me and Jeannie, and they are, or can be, Eurydice and Medusa – yeah, picture this – they're the women of the myths! The women who were given gazes, as weapons or as death sentences, by the gods for whom they were playthings. They are, or can be, Eurydice and Medusa, and they are, or can be, me and Jeannie, and so it occurs again, or must occur.

The grieving self, in Jones's book, is plural, malleable, neither one nor the other, but existing somewhere in between. Indeed, it is this between-space (both formally and thematically) that the book inhabits, directs and curates – tiptoes around – but also expresses with remarkable precision. The instance of the immobilising gaze, which is at once the instance of trauma and the instance of the splitting of the self, 'vanishes upon remembering [...] To articulate her is to lose her'. The creation of Jeannie, then, acts as a kind of defence against the horror of articulation-obliteration. Jeannie is like the mirror you might hold up to the gaze of the Medusa, or the punctured paper you might hold up to an eclipse: deflecting it, looking at it only slantways, the thing itself remaining inarticulable but at least alive.

I could quote at length those sections of the book which demonstrate Jones's surprising and original mastery of voice. Sentences are breath-less, full, expertly controlled, moving: 'Tucking her hair behind her ear like she does, saying, What?, like maybe what she really heard was "sighed" or "cried" or "come outside",' and 'It's one moment that is connected to all the other moments that you brought it into, all by yourself, and when you think about it you connect them all togeth-er and you light them up, a constellation.' Again and again, Jones does not let her language rest into easy or neat rhythms, but wrangles it, plies it into shape, interrogates it, allows it to run on and repeat when the 'rules' of writing might suggest this to be inappropriate. Whole sections of the work do this. One episode, 'All the Holes' — in which Jeannie goes on a Tinder date — draws together one of the abiding images throughout the book: the image of a hole puncturing a smooth surface. 'You must be hard and unmoving,' Jones writes, in the early chapter 'Snakes', 'because even a very small hole could cause all your insides to leak out and congeal, exposed.' Later, the lilies that Jeannie walks past on her way to work act as a point of puncture, a hole in the fabric of space and time: 'The flower stand is a pin that, when Jeannie passes it, pokes a little hole right through now and into her parents' living room ten years ago. The smell of lilies reminds Jeannie that grief is elastic.' And finally, in 'All the Holes', Jeannie enacts a pantomime of womanhood as she prepares for her date, 'bending forward to pull up stockings, bending right and left to dab perfume on knobs of wrists [...] squatting by the mirror to apply, carefully, a face'. She allows her date to mistake her lonely need to be filled ('to have all the holes in her self and in her body filled with solid things') for lust, before the episode explodes into a joyful destruction, a ripping apart of the performance of gender, a violent 'holing' of the smooth surface of language: 'Shedding not identifiers, but language, language itself — the liberation! Jeannie sweeps away syntax and her body fades.'

Something to Be Tiptoed Around is an original, arresting contribution to feminist writing, to writing trauma, and a deeply moving exploration of grief and loss. 'Grief is not the aftermath of death: it is death. It is death, infecting life,' writes Jones. There are not many who could send forth an emissary like Jeannie to the underworld, and have them report back with such candour and beauty.

Dr Elizabeth Macfarlane
Creative Writing Program
The University of Melbourne
2018

Page Notes

The page notes anchor *Something to Be Tiptoed Around* to its scholarly and literary sources. The notes are organised by author, and subsequently by authors' works. Bolded text is by Jones, and inverted commas in her text indicate that *Something to Be Tiptoed Around* quotes a source directly; the absence of inverted commas indicates that the page note refers to a key concept or trope in a source. Where space allows, an extended quotation is given from the original source, to provide context. For more information about the page notes, see the Notes on the Genre.

BERGER, JOHN:

Ways of Seeing. **London: Penguin Books, 1973.**

Page 52: her inward-turned self forced outward, forced now to be the object of a hungry and licentious gaze. (47: 'One might simplify this by saying: men act and women appear. Men look at women. Women watch themselves being looked at. This determines not only most relations between men and women but also the relation of women to themselves. The surveyor of woman in herself is male: the surveyed female. Thus she turns herself into an object — and most particularly an object of vision: a sight.')

BUTLER, JUDITH:

Gender Trouble: Feminism and the Subversion of Identity. Edited by Linda J. Nicholson. New York: Routledge, 1990.

'Bracha's Eurydice.' Foreword. In *The Matrixial Borderspace*, vii–xii. Minneapolis: The University of Minnesota Press, 2006.

Pages xv–xvi: 'She is presented … nullify the loss.'[…] 'We were not supposed … unambiguous life.' […] 'We turned around, needing … capture her that way…' […] 'and when we sought to have her through knowing her, we lost her.' […] 'we lost her, since … instant that is preserved.' (All from 2006, viii: 'No, she is presented there, and so she acquires a certain presence, but the presence does not redeem the loss, the presence does not nullify the loss. We were not supposed to look back to what may not be seen, but we did; we broke a law, a law that would have mandated that we look only and always forward to unambiguous life. We turned around, needing to know, but it was this need, to know, to know with certainty, that undid us, for we could not capture her that way. And when we sought to have her through knowing her, we lost her, since she cannot be had that way. But nevertheless it is this instant that is preserved… .')

Page xvii: 'A temporality in which … continuous, trauma.' (2006, ix: 'a psychic landscape that gives itself as partial object, as grains and crumbs, as she puts it, as remnants that are, on the one hand, the result, the scattered effects of an unknowable history of trauma, the trauma that others who precede us have lived through and, on the other hand, the very sites in which a new possibility for visual experience emerges, one that establishes a temporality in which the past is not past but is not present, in which the present emerges, but from the scattered and animated remains of a continuing, though not continuous, trauma.')

Page 15: It's a duality triggered by trauma. (2006, viii: 'A realm of appearance… .')

Page 24: At all of those times, you have added an extra layer to that moment, a filter, a wrapper, a trace. (2006, xi)

Page 25: 'A temporality in which ... continuous, trauma.'
(2006, ix: 'a psychic landscape that gives itself as partial object, as grains and crumbs, as she puts it, as remnants that are, on the one hand, the result, the scattered effects of an unknowable history of trauma, the trauma that others who precede us have lived through and, on the other hand, the very sites in which a new possibility for visual experience emerges, one that establishes a temporality in which the past is not past but is not present, in which the present emerges, but from the scattered and animated remains of a continuing, though not continuous, trauma.')

Page 27: 'The trace, the sign ... beauty itself.' (2006, xii: 'And the trace, the sign of loss, the remnant of loss, is understood as the link, the occasional and nearly impossible connection, between trauma and beauty itself.')

To articulate it is to lose it. ...to articulate her is to lose her. (Both from 2006, xii)

Pages 28, 30: 'She is presented ... nullify the loss.' [...] 'We were not supposed ... unambiguous life.' [...] 'We turned around, needing ... capture her that way...' [...] 'and when we sought to have her through knowing her, we lost her.' [...] 'we lost her, since ... instant that is preserved.' (All from 2006, viii: 'No, she is presented there, and so she acquires a certain presence, but the presence does not redeem the loss, the presence does not nullify the loss. We were not supposed to look back to what may not be seen, but we did; we broke a law, a law that would have mandated that we look only and always forward to unambiguous life. We turned around, needing to know, but it was this need, to know, to know with certainty, that undid us, for we could not capture her that way. And when we sought to have her through knowing her, we lost her, since she cannot be had that way. But nevertheless it is this instant that is preserved... .')

Page 45: And so: the looking back captures (2006, viii)

Page 46: Fleeting and permanent, a gaze that happens once forever and over and over again in a new measure of time. (2006, xii: 'Our gaze pushes her back to death, since we are prohibited from looking, and we know that by looking, we will lose her. And we will not lose her for the first time, but we will lose her again, and it will be by virtue of our own gaze…'.)

When Eurydice is looked at, she ceases to be — and yet, in the moment she's looked at, she's corporeal, apprehensible. (2006, p. viii: 'in the very act of seeing, we lose.')

Page 47: 'As in a hall of mirrors, her image is redoubled and there seems to be a set of them, all of them fading and appearing at once.' (2006, viii: 'Her image is redoubled, and there seems to be a set of them, all of them fading and appearing at one.')

Page 53: But the body is just language… (1990, 136)

Jeannie's reduced to her fucked-up pantomime: a vacant body, a painted, panting doll (1990, 25).

Doing this, Jeannie rejects the self-imposed order inherent in concepts of identity and recognition and individuation, she rejects the assumption that she is distinct… that she is one thing or another thing and that she must be recognised that way: (2006, x)

Pages 53-54: I mean, if the body's just language… (1990, 136).

Page 66: She has passed over that threshold into death and all that is left of her is the trace, the remnant of loss… (2006, xii)

Page 68: traces, remnants and links of memory slipping away as we tug at the thread… (2006, xi-xii).

Page 74: self-mirroring landscape (2006, viii).

Page 75: 'see her, redoubled, a thousand Jeannies fading and appearing all at once?' (2006, viii)

CIXOUS, HÉLÈNE:

'The Laugh of the Medusa.' Translated by Keith Cohen and Paula Cohen. *Signs: Journal of Women in Culture and Society* 1, no. 4. (Summer, 1976): 875–893.

Page xiii: 'a locus where the repression of women has been perpetuated, over and over, more or less consciously …

where woman has never her turn to speak' [...] 'all the more serious and unpardonable in that writing is precisely the very possibility of change, the space that can serve as a springboard for subversive thought'. (879)

Page 7: Snakes that whispered into infinity… (889: 'she goes and passes into infinity.')

Page 9: Cixous represents her in a new space, a space where she can behave like hot wax, where she can seep and spread. (876: 'I wished that that woman would write and proclaim this unique empire so that other women, other unacknowledged sovereigns, might exclaim: I, too, overflow; my desires have invented new desires, my body knows unheard-of songs. Time and again I, too, have felt so full of luminous torrents that I could burst – burst with forms much more beautiful than those which are put up in frames and sold for a stinking fortune.')

She's everywhere. (878: 'What happiness for us who are omitted, brushed aside at the scene of inheritances; we inspire ourselves and we expire without running out of breath, we are everywhere!')

For Cixous, Medusa's body is endless and unsevered; it's one long thread. (878: 'our blood flows and we extend ourselves without ever reaching an end…')

Laughing, Medusa becomes… (885: 'You only have to look at the Medusa straight on to see her. And she's not deadly. She's beautiful and she's laughing.')

Our identities are chaotic, multiple, alterable and infinite. (883: 'A process of different subjects knowing one another and beginning one another anew only from the living boundaries of the other: a multiple and inexhaustible course with millions of encounters and transformations of the same into the other and into the in-between, from which woman takes her form…'; 889: '…this gift of alterability.')

Page 47: 'She becomes infinite, and she transcends and spans: like Cixous's Medusa, Eurydice … becomes several.' (889: '… she goes and passes into infinity. [...] When id is ambiguously uttered—the wonder of being several – she doesn't defend herself against these unknown women whom she's surprised at becoming, but derives pleasure from this gift of alterability.')

Page 53: flight into freedom and infinity... (889: 'she goes and passes into infinity.')

Jeannie transcends semiotics, becomes fluid, several, infinite (889: 'the wonder of being several...'; 876: 'Where is the ebullient, infinite woman...')

ETTINGER, BRACHA:

The Matrixial Borderspace. **Edited by Brian Massumi. Minneapolis: University of Minnesota Press, 2006.**

Page 46: They carry each other's burdens, they unify each other's myths. The encounter that they're locked in and its process of becoming cancel out the power of the unwanted, ordered gaze that would reject and destroy them. (89: 'traces of trauma are dispersed between several partners, and what binds one partial subject can open the eyes of another partial-subject.')

Page 65: In the underworld, Jeannie carries the burden of my trauma for me, she bears witness to my trauma. The gaze touches: (141: 'Since I cannot fully handle events that profoundly concern me, they fade-in-transformation while my non-I becomes with(h)ness to them. It may happen that because of my premature subjectivity or the highly traumatic value of the events, I cannot psychically handle my encounters at all. [...] Thus my others will process traumatic events for me...')

Page 66: my proxy, my envoy, a witness to my rage and grief. (141: 'Since I cannot fully handle events that profoundly concern me, they fade-in-transformation while my non-I becomes with(h)ness to them.')

FREUD, SIGMUND:

'Mourning and Melancholia.' In *The Standard Edition of the Complete Psychological Works of Sigmund Freud, Volume XIV*

(1914–1916): On the History of the Psycho-Analytic Movement, Papers on Metapsychology and Other Works, 243–258. Edited by James Strachey and Anna Freud. London: The Hogarth Press and the Institute of Psychoanalysis, 1957.

Page 15: 'A reflexive turning away, in the face of loss, from all that isn't loss itself...' (244: 'A reflexive turning away, in the face of loss, from all that isn't loss itself.')

GIBBS, ANNA:

'Fictocriticism, Affect, Mimesis: Engendering Differences.' TEXT: *Journal of the Australian Association of Writing Programs* 9, no. 1 (April 2005). http://www.textjournal.com.au/april05/gibbs.htm

Page xiv: as a polyphonic, discordant writing – a 'haunted writing', which is to say, a writing haunted by itself – fictocriticism is a writing Gibbs says is 'traced by numerous voices,' ('I want to begin by suggesting that fictocriticism is a "haunted writing" ... traced by numerous voices which work now in unison, at other times in counterpoint, and others still against each other, in deliberate discord.')

existing discourse as rigid and unchanging as though it were set in stone. ('The problem of haunted writing comes to the fore in academic discourse when disciplinary authority and discursive protocol function as the voice of the dead stalking the present so as to paralyse it with terror, or else as a kind of watchful superego as resistant to modification as if it were a text inscribed in stone.')

fictocritical writing does not aim to *make* a point; it aims to *have* a point. ('It aims not simply to make a point but have a point – which is to bring about a certain change in a certain set of narrative relations.'

HARRISON, JANE ELLEN:

Prolegomena to the Study of Greek Religion. New Jersey: Princeton University Press, 1908.

Page 8: Poor Medusa, without agency, robbed even of her ability to look. Her potency recognised by legend and her beauty by culture only after her head was severed – but what of her body? (187: 'It is equally apparent that in her essence Medusa is a head and nothing more; her potency only begins when her head is severed, and that potency resides in the head; she is in a word a mask with a body later appended.')

KRISTEVA, JULIA:

Powers of Horror: An Essay on Abjection. **Translated by Leon S. Roudiez. New York: Columbia University Press, 1982.**

Page xvii: 'It is death, infecting life,' (4).

Page 15: It's a demarcation by the self and of the self. (10: 'when I seek (myself), lose (myself), or experience jouissance – then "I" is heterogeneous. Discomfort, unease, dizziness stemming from an ambiguity that, through the violence of a revolt against, demarcates a space out of which signs and objects arise.')

Page 25: 'It is death, infecting life.' (4: 'The corpse, seen without God and outside of science, is the utmost of abjection. It is death infecting life.')

Page 34: When we see death and its accessories, something happens. It prompts a delineation of self, a small and silent and subconscious SOS signal, a setting of coordinates, a mapping and positioning of the self, a quiet motion that could be for comfort or survival ... When we are confronted with death in this way – looking at it, really looking at *it* itself, its physical manifestation – our own physical selves are positioned on the very border of their statuses as living beings. (3: 'These body fluids, this defilement, this shit are what life withstands, hardly and with difficulty, on the part of death. There, I am at the border of my condition as a living being. My body extricates itself, as being alive, from that border.')

Our minds recoil so violently and so decisively from such borders that they create little chambers within themselves to house such horrors. (10: 'Discomfort, unease, dizziness stemming from an ambiguity that, through the violence of

92

a revolt against, demarcates a space out of which signs and objects arise. Thus braided, woven, ambivalent, a heterogeneous flux marks out a territory that I can call my own...').

Page 46: Jeannie and Medusa, Harriet and Eurydice are mimetic, braided, fused. (10: 'Obviously, I am only like someone else: mimetic logic of the advent of the ego, objects, and signs.' 'Thus braided, woven, ambivalent, a heterogeneous flux marks out a territory that I can call my own because the Other, having dwelt in me as alter ego, points it out to me through loathing.')

Page 62: even as I expel her in an act of revulsion... (3: 'But since the food is not an "other" for "me," who am only in their desire, I expel myself, I spit myself out, I abject myself within the same motion through which "I" claim to establish myself.')

a discharge of the part of myself that's grieving and can only exist outside of the parts of myself that aren't... (2: 'Without a sign (for him), it beseeches a discharge, a convulsion, a crying out.')

Page 74: Suspended amniotic in this way, Jeannie's on the border. Jeannie's neither conscious nor unconscious... (7: 'Since they make the conscious/unconscious distinction irrelevant, borderline subjects and their speech constitute propitious ground for a sublimating discourse ("aes- thet-ic" or "mystical," etc.), rather than a scientific or rationalist one.'; 11: 'On such limits and at the limit one could say that there is no unconscious, which is elaborated when representations and affects (whether or not tied to representations) shape a logic. Here, on the contrary, consciousness has not assumed its rights and transformed into signifiers those fluid demarcations of yet unstable territories where an "I" that is taking shape is ceaselessly straying.')

ejected and dejected, she must write her own... (8: 'The one by whom the abject exists is thus a deject who places (himself), separates (himself), situates (himself), and therefore strays instead of getting his bearings, desiring, belonging, or refusing.')

Page 75: Jeannie never stops marking off boundaries of her universe, but I'm always moving them. They're unknowable

and fluid. [...] When your whole world, and your whole existence in it, is defined by something fractured, you must constantly question your solidity. You must quiver like a distant object in a heatwave, you must fluctuate. (8: 'A deviser of territories, languages, works, the deject never stops demarcating his universe whose fluid confines — for they are constituted of a non-object, the abject — constantly question his solidity and impel him to start afresh.')

Page 84: 'It is death, infecting life,' (4).

POLLOCK, GRISELDA:

'Femininity: Aporia or Sexual Difference?' Introduction. In *The Matrixial Borderspace*, pp. 1–38. Minneapolis: The University of Minnesota Press, 2006.

Page 46: Meeting at this shared pin on the map... (3).

Page 53: Turning inward on herself as she does, Jeannie wins her body back by shedding it: by outgrowing language, by leaving it behind; by pluralising her self and the meaning of her self over and over again. [...] Shunning signifiers, ceasing to place meaning inside them and so stripping them of worth, killing them, laying them waste... (3).

Page 62: That's the ironic part of having broken myself into two ... Me and Jeannie, Jeannie and me: our reflexive, shattered selfhood is a fleeting encounter occurring at a shared borderspace, (3: 'Ettinger invites us to consider aspects of subjectivity as encounter occurring at shared borderspaces between several co-affecting partial-subjectivities that are never entirely fused or totally lost, but share and process, within an always-already minimal difference, elements of each unknown other.')

Page 65: The self and the other are two fragments of one whole: two partial, shattered pieces that are never really joined together but never really broken quite apart. (3).

Page 74: to seek what we — what I — have lost... (2).

TUMARKIN, MARIA:

Traumascapes. Melbourne: Melbourne University Press, 2005.

Pages xvi–xvii: 'The past enters the present as an intruder, an unwelcome guest...' (12: 'The past enters the present as an intruder, an unwelcome guest';) **the knot tying the two together can be loosened but will not, cannot be untied** (p. 14: 'At traumascapes, the knot tying the present and the past together often cannot be untied.')

Page 25: 'The past enters the present as an intruder, an unwelcome guest...' (12: 'The past enters the present as an intruder, an unwelcome guest';) **the knot tying the two together can be loosened but will not, cannot be untied** (p. 14: 'At traumascapes, the knot tying the present and the past together often cannot be untied.')

Page 57: When Jeannie tries to remember the days that came afterward, all she gets is a formless lump, that when she pokes it spews out tiny pieces without syntax... (11).

NIETZSCHE, FRIEDRICH:

On the Genealogy of Morals. **Edited, with commentary, by Walter Kaufmann. Translated by Walter Kaufmann and R. J. Hollingdale. New York: Vintage Books, 1989.**

Page 52: There is no being behind doing, effecting, becoming... (45: 'But there is no such substratum; there is no "being" behind the doing, acting, becoming; "the doer" is merely a fiction added to the deed — the deed is everything.')

MASSUMI, BRIAN:

'Painting: The Voice of the Grain.' Afterword. In *The Matrixial Borderspace*, pp. 201–212. Minneapolis: University of Minnesota Press, 2005.

Page 46: The encounter that they're locked in and its process of becoming cancel out the power of the unwanted, ordered gaze that would reject and destroy them. (211)

Bibliography

Berger, John. *Ways of Seeing*. London: Penguin Books, 1973.

Butler, Judith. 'Bracha's Eurydice.' Foreword. In *The Matrixial Borderspace*, vii–xii. Edited by Brian Massumi. Minneapolis: The University of Minnesota Press, 2006.

———. *Gender Trouble: Feminism and the Subversion of Identity*. Edited by Linda J. Nicholson. New York: Routledge, 1990.

Cixous, Hélène. 'The Laugh of the Medusa.' Translated by Keith Cohen and Paula Cohen. *Signs: Journal of Women in Culture and Society* 1, no. 4. (Summer, 1976): 875–893.

Ettinger, Bracha. *The Matrixial Borderspace*. Edited by Brian Massumi. Minneapolis: University of Minnesota Press, 2006.

Freud, Sigmund. 'Mourning and Melancholia.' In *The Standard Edition of the Complete Psychological Works of Sigmund Freud, Volume XIV (1914–1916): On the History of the Psycho-Analytic Movement, Papers on Metapsychology and Other Works*, 243–258. Edited by James Strachey and Anna Freud. London: The Hogarth Press and the Institute of Psychoanalysis, 1957.

Fuss, Diana and Joel Sanders. 'Berggasse 19: Inside Freud's Office.' In *Stud: Architectures of Masculinity*, 112–139. Edited by Joel Sanders. New York: Princeton Architectural Press, 1996.

Garber, Marjorie, and Nancy Vickers, editors. *The Medusa Reader*. New York: Routledge, 2003.

Gibbs, Anna. 'Fictocriticism, Affect, Mimesis: Engendering Differences.' *TEXT Journal* 9, no. 1 (April 2005). Brisbane: Griffith University, 2005. http://www.textjournal.com.au/april05/gibbs.htm

Harrison, Jane Ellen. *Prolegomena to the Study of Greek Religion*. New Jersey: Princeton University Press, 1908.

Jones, Emma Marie. 'Something To Be Tiptoed Around Until It Goes Away: On The Abjection And Matrixiality Of Grief And Subjectivity.' Master's thesis., University of Melbourne, 2015.

Kristeva, Julia. *Powers of Horror: An Essay on Abjection*. Translated by Leon S. Roudiez. New York: Columbia University Press, 1982.

Lacan, Jacques. *Freud's Papers on Technique 1953–1954: The Seminar of Jacques Lacan, Book 1*. Edited by Jacques-Alain Miller. Translated by John Forrester. New York: Norton, 1991.

Massumi, Brian. 'Painting: The Voice of the Grain.' Afterword. In *The Matrixial Borderspace*, 201–212. Edited by Brian Massumi. Minneapolis: University of Minnesota Press, 2005.

Nietzsche, Friedrich W. On the Genealogy of Morals. Edited, with commentary, by Walter Kaufmann. Translated by Walter Kaufmann and R. J. Hollingdale. New York: Vintage Books, 1989.

Ovid. *Metamorphoses: Book I–VIII*. Translated by Frank Justus Miller. London: William Heinemann, 1951.

Ovid. *Metamorphoses: Book VIII–XV*. Translated by Henry Thomas Riley. London: George Bell & Sons, 1893.

Pollock, Griselda. 'Femininity: Aporia or Sexual Difference?' Introduction. In *The Matrixial Borderspace*, 5–65. Edited by Brian Massumi. Minneapolis: University of Minnesota Press, 2006.

Seal, Mark. 'Gianni Versace: from "The Versace Moment" by Mark Seal (1996).' in *The Medusa Reader*, edited by Marjorie Garber and Nancy Vickers, 276. UK: Routledge, 2003.

Tumarkin, Maria. *Traumascapes: The Power and Fate of Places Transformed by Tragedy*. Melbourne: Melbourne University Press, 2005.

Acknowledgements

I owe thanks to so many for a book so small! To my editors, Aaron Mannion and Ellie Atack — thank you for your patience, your willingness and your openness. To Sybil Nolan, a puller of many strings. To the team at Grattan Street Press, many of whom I haven't met, but all of whom have worked to make this little book tangible: thank you.

Elizabeth Macfarlane, thank you for all you've given to me and this project that has been so valuable: your time, your wisdom, your encouragement and your pep talks. Ronnie Scott, for your careful supervision of the thesis that this book once was, I am grateful.

To Annabel at *The Lifted Brow* for publishing an excerpt of this manuscript in its print issue in 2017, for wonderfully editing those parts of it, and for kindly encouraging me to repurpose it now, thank you. To those at Scribe who judged my work worthy of being shortlisted for the Nonfiction Prize for Young Writers in 2015 — thank you — what a drive forward that merit has been.

Thanks, Sean, for taking the pictures.

So many of my friends have read parts of this manuscript as it has evolved. Special thanks to Eloise, Sian and Paul for comments, edits and welcome distraction.

My nest friends, for being my Melbourne family — Carina, Dan, Emma, Imo, Isabelle, Jake, Josh, Maddie, Mark, Pete, Reece, Sca, Sean, Troy, Vinnie, all of you — thank you.

Matt, for everything, thank you.

And to my family, to Mum, Dad and Reilly — thank you for loving and supporting me and each other, through loss and through life.

Staff Acknowledgements

The original concept for the Grattan Street Shorts series was created by publishing students who worked at Grattan Street Press in semester 2, 2017, and their successors turned the concept into reality. Creating a new series is exciting, but it also involves putting hard boundaries around wonderful, airy ideas; boundaries that create a distinct editorial identity sufficiently interesting and reproducible to sustain a series through many iterations. The process requires a challenging set of aesthetic and technical decisions, followed by skilful application of editing, design and production knowhow. Congratulations, then, to the group of students who worked on *Something to Be Tiptoed Around*, and who have created an attractive, impactful book that is an excellent model for those to follow: Ellie Atack (editor), Angela Iaria (cover design) and Beth Wentworth (production editor and typesetter). Thanks also to Mark Davis, who created the internal design and gave helpful feedback on the cover, and Aaron Mannion, who oversaw the conceptual stage in 2017 and led the editing in semester 1, 2018. Thanks, too, to

Elizabeth Macfarlane, our colleague in Creative Writing, who created the accompanying commentary, and to freelance photographer Sean Barnes, whose wonderful photograph of lilies was a self-selecting choice for the book's cover. Thanks also to Kerin Forstmanis, who wrangled the contracts for us, and to our printers Ingram Spark, as usual.

Of course, this book would have been nothing without Emma Marie Jones and her wonderful manuscript, so thanks first and last to her.

Sybil Nolan
Coordinator, Grattan Street Press

Grattan Street Press Personnel

Semester 1, 2018

Editing and Proofreading
Grayce Arlov, Ellie Atack, Luke Fussell, Jessica Hall, Stephanie Lightfoot, Beth Wentworth

Design and Production
Ellen Dutton, Angela Iaria, Alexandra Robson, Beth Wentworth

Sales and Marketing
Jessica Allan, Brooke Munday, Audrey Whybrow

Social Media
Cherry Cai, Georgia Gallo

Submissions Officers
Ellie Atack, Laura Bianca Cesile, Katie Hollister, Sunniva Midtskogen, Audrey Whybrow

Website and Blogs
Laura Bianca Cesile, Katie Hollister, Sunniva Midtskogen, Georgia Quirke-Luping

Academic Staff
Mark Davis, Katherine Day, Aaron Mannion, Sybil Nolan

About Grattan Street Press

Grattan Street Press is a trade publisher based in Melbourne. A start-up press, we aim to publish a range of work, including contemporary literature, trade non-fiction, and children's books, and to re-publish culturally valuable works that are out of print. The press is an initiative of the Publishing and Communications program in the School of Culture and Communication at the University of Melbourne, and is staffed by graduate students, who receive hands-on experience of every aspect of the publication process.

The press is a not-for-profit organisation that seeks to build long-term relationships within the Australian literary and publishing community. We also partner with community organisations in Melbourne and beyond to co-publish books that contribute to public knowledge and discussion.

Organisations interested in partnering with us can contact us at coordinator@grattanstreetpress. com. Writers interested in submitting a manuscript to the Grattan Street Shorts series can contact us at editorial@grattanstreetpress.com.

www.ingramcontent.com/pod-product-compliance
Ingram Content Group Australia Pty Ltd
76 Discovery Rd, Dandenong South VIC 3175, AU
AUHW010825050325
407891AU00006B/40

9 780987 625380